WAIT FOR ME

STUDY GUIDE

Discover the
Power of Purity

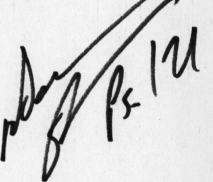

NELSON REFERENCE & ELECTRONIC
A Division of Thomas Nelson Publishers
Since 1798
www.thomasnelson.com

Published by Thomas Nelson, Inc., P.O. Box 141000, Nashville, TN, 37214.

All Scripture quotations are taken from The Holy Bible, New Century Version®.
Copyright© 1987, 1988, 1991 by Word Publishing, a Division of Thomas Nelson,
Inc. Used by permission. All rights reserved.

ISBN 1-4185-0195-6

Printed in the United States of America
05 06 07 08 09 RRD 9 8 7 6 5 4 3 2 1

CONTENTS

Wait for Me

by Rebecca St. James

Darling, did you know that I
I dream about you
Waiting for the look in your eyes
When we meet for the first time
Darling, did you know that I
I pray about you
Praying that you will hold on
Keep your loving eyes only for me

I am waiting for
Praying for you, darling
Wait for me too
Wait for me as I wait for you
I am waiting for
Praying for you, darling
Wait for me too
Wait for me as I wait for you
Darling, wait

Darling, did you know I dream about life together
Knowing it will be forever
I'll be yours and you'll be mine
And darling, when I say
'Til death do us part

I'll mean it with all of my heart
Now and always, faithful to you

I am waiting for
Praying for you, darling
Wait for me too
Wait for me as I wait for you
I am waiting for
Praying for you, darling
Wait for me too
Wait for me as I wait for you
Darling, wait

Now I know you may have made mistakes
But there's forgiveness and a second chance
So wait for me darling
Wait for me
Wait for me

I am waiting for
Praying for you, darling
Wait for me too
Wait for me as I wait for you
I am waiting for
Praying for you, darling
Wait for me too
Wait for me as I wait for you
Darling, wait

LESSON 1

Learning to Dream

Reflect

I believe that God has placed 'The Dream' inside every woman, unless He has specifically called you to singleness. We each have a desire for intimacy, for someone to know us fully and love us completely. We long to be able to share our hearts and still find acceptance.

What dreams do you have about your future spouse? How do you imagine meeting him? What do you think he'll be like?

_____

_____

_____

_____

What about marriage do you most look forward to?

_____

_____

_____

Thoughts

Dreams are one of the most exciting gifts that God has given us. I dream all the time—about what my life will be like in future years, about what I'll do

1

with friends and family over holidays, even about what I'll do over the weekend. And of course I dream about who I'll marry and what he'll be like.

But the most beautiful dreams we can have are not those we make up for ourselves. The incredible truth is that God dreams about *me*. The Bible says that before I was even born, God was thinking about me.

> "LORD, *you have examined me and know all about me. You know when I sit down and when I get up. You know my thoughts before I think them . . . You made my whole being; you formed me in my mother's body . . . you saw my body as it was formed. All the days planned for me were written in your book before I was one day old. God, your thoughts are precious to me. They are so many! If I could count them, they would be more than all the grains of sand. When I wake up, I am still with you."*
> —PSALM 139:1, 2, 13, 16–18 NCV

Psalm 139 is one of my favorite passages in the Bible. It amazes me to think that God knows everything about me, that He knows everything I do, and that He was dreaming and planning for me before I was even born. It's easy for us to forget how deeply and personally God loves us. Of course there are general things that He dreams of for everyone, like knowing Him and being holy—but did you ever think about what God dreams for you personally? Why did He make you exactly the way you are? Why do you love piano or comedies or books? Why are you shy or talkative or funny? Did you ever think that God might have made you that way for a reason—that who you are and the way you are is part of the dreams He has for your life?

What do you think God enjoys about you?

_____

_____

_____

As a single woman, you can only wonder about the man you will someday marry. But God knows exactly who he is. He designed everything about him, from his hair color to the smallest quirks of his character. God knows exactly what challenges you will face in your life together, every romantic moment you'll enjoy together and every fight you'll struggle through. Just think how amazing our dreams would be if instead of making them up for ourselves, we asked God to give us a glimpse of His dreams for us. Those dreams have all the benefit of being true and all the certainty of being fulfilled.

What dreams do you believe God has given you for your marriage?

_____

_____

_____

What is the hardest part about waiting for these dreams to be fulfilled?

_____

_____

_____

Many women find it hard to believe that the dream God has planned for them is so much more exciting than anything the world has to offer or what they could dream for themselves.

The dreams that God has for all of us are perfect! They're a perfect blend of how He designed us, and the role He has for us in His kingdom. They're the combination of everything that we are and everything that we have to offer to Him and to each other. When we follow His dreams for our lives, we truly live in hope and expectation. We can't even guess what adventures He has waiting for us just around the corner. We don't have to live with fear or regrets because we know that He is always taking care of us, and He can use even our mistakes to further the dream He has for us. When we pursue God's dreams for us, then we can truly live life to the fullest!

"A thief comes to steal and kill and destroy, but I came to give life—life in all its fullness."

—JOHN 10:10 NCV

As we learn to envision the dream God has for us, we can rise above the empty dreams that the world offers us. Instead of getting caught up in a lie, we can live freely in the truth of who God created us to be and all that He calls us to do. We no longer have to be afraid that our dreams will never be fulfilled because we know that they're safe in our Father's keeping.

Great Love Stories: Isaac and Rebekah

The Scene:
Abraham spent most of his life dreaming of being a father. When he and his wife were still a relatively young couple, God had promised him a son—and not just any son, either. God also promised Abraham that he would father a nation, God's own chosen people. It took God a long time to fulfill His promise, but at last Isaac—Abraham's son of promise—was born. Now, however, Abraham had other problems. He had a son, but he couldn't become the father of a nation until that son got married. And how could Isaac's children grow up to be God's chosen nation if Isaac married an ungodly, unbelieving, Canaanite woman from the land where Abraham and his family were living now? Abraham could think of only one solution—he had to find a wife for Isaac from his own people, back in his hometown.

As was the custom in those days, Abraham sent a servant to find a girl and arrange the marriage. It was a pretty easy arrangement for Isaac—all he had to do was sit and wait for his bride to come along. The hard part of this task was put on the servant. However, it was an easy task for God.

The Story:
Read Genesis 24:10–67.

How would you feel if a stranger told you that God had chosen you to be the wife of a man you'd never met?

- scared
- excited
- nervous
- surprised
- happy
- doubtful
- shocked
- special
- worried
- uncertain
- accepting

● other:

_____

_____

_____

_____

We don't usually imagine arranged marriages as very romantic. But I think this is one of the most beautiful and passionate pictures in the entire Bible: the moment when Isaac looks up from his evening prayers and sees his future wife coming to meet him for the first time. Neither of them really understands it yet, but they have truly been chosen and created for each other. The story of how the servant finds Rebekah makes it clear: God chose this woman for Isaac's wife long before she ever dreamed of him.

I wonder what Rebekah was thinking as she listened to the servant relate the story of his commission from Abraham and his prayer to God. How must she have felt as she realized that God had chosen her to be the wife of a man she'd never even heard of? Think of the courage it took for her to accept God's dream for her, to leave her family and home—perhaps never to see them again—for the unknown adventure ahead of her.

We like to think of dreams as our own, the fulfillment of what we want for ourselves. But the greatest dream and the greatest adventure is the one we experience when we get caught up in the dream that God planned for us before we were even born. His dreams are so big that we can never entirely understand them, but we're still called to play a part in them. That's the dream that Rebekah was realizing as she climbed on a camel for a ride across the desert into an unknown future. That's the dream that I want to long for. That's the dream we can be certain will come true.

Do you pray for your future husband? What do you pray for him?

_____

_____

_____

_____

_____

What is the hardest part for you about trusting God's dreams for your future?

_____

_____

_____

_____

_____

_____

_____

_____

Quiz:
Are You a Dreamer?

How much do you dream about the future? Are you so caught up in your own dreams that it's hard to listen to God's ideas? Or are you so down-to-earth and realistic that it's hard for you to imagine the adventures God has for you?

1. What do you want to be when you grow up?
    a. Rich, famous, successful, godly, and happy
    b. The best at something I love
    c. Just happy
    d. Do I have to grow up?

2. What do you most look forward to right now?
    a. Growing up, getting married, having a job and a family I love
    b. Graduating from college and entering "the real world"
    c. Finishing my next test
    d. The weekend!

3. How much time do you spend daydreaming?
    a. I'm very focused on the here and now.
    b. I daydream right before I fall asleep at night.
    c. My friends and I are always talking about our dreams and plans.
    d. What did you say? I wasn't paying attention.

4. What aspect of your future husband do you think about the most?
    a. The way he will look
    b. The way he will treat me
    c. The way I'll treat him
    d. I've never thought about it.

5. How much of your wedding do you have planned?
    a. I've never given it a second thought.
    b. I noticed a couple of good ideas at my cousin's wedding.
    c. I've figured out just about everything, except the groom!
    d. I've planned the whole thing, and I even made a mix of romantic tunes for the wedding night.

Letter to My Future Spouse

$\mathcal{D}$earest,

As I'm dreaming of you, I know that God has given me desires and dreams that will someday be fulfilled in you. I am dreaming and praying for you that . . .

I am trusting God for you by . . .

Learning to Surrender

Reflect

Isn't it just like the Lord to invite me
To put all my dreams in His hands
Forever releasing the grip that once held them
Forever surrendering my plans?

Thoughts

Sometimes women prevent their dreams from being realized by holding onto them too tightly. But the more we cling to them, the more we destroy them. The dreams that God meant to be beautiful can easily become twisted and broken by our past, our culture, and our inability to let go.

The world tells us that if we believe in our dreams then we have to make them happen. But God promises that He will fulfill the dreams He has for us—in His perfect way and in His perfect timing. Only then will they become dreams that are worth living.

Look up the word "surrender" in your dictionary and write it's meaning here.

_____

_____

_____

If you were to surrender your dreams completely to God, what would the outcome be?

_____

_____

_____

_____

_____

_____

"Those people who know they have great spiritual needs are happy, because the kingdom of heaven belongs to them."

—MATTHEW 5:3 NCV

All through the Bible, you can see the amazing upside-downness of how God runs His kingdom. God seems to delight in upending the natural order of how things work. An old, barren man becomes the father of many nations; a young, deceitful son becomes the inheritor of a promise; an immoral Samaritan woman becomes the first foreign missionary; an uneducated, unreliable fisherman become the cornerstone of the church. The only thing these people have in common is their need for God and their willingness to surrender.

"I tell you the truth, a grain of wheat must fall to the ground and die to make many seeds. But if it never dies, it remains only a single seed."

—JOHN 12:24 NCV

"When you sow a seed, it must die in the ground before it can live and grow."

—1 CORINTHIANS 15:36 NCV

Surrender is a lot like death. The loss hurts, and it's hard. It requires giving up everything you dreamed about for the future. But the beauty of surrender is that God promises a resurrection—and the revival of the dream is much more beautiful than anything you could imagine on your own. It's not until we are willing to give up our dreams that God is able to reset and restart our dreams, transforming them beyond all hope.

In what ways have your past experiences influenced your thinking about God's plans for you?

_____

_____

Do you think the culture has shaped your way of dreaming? If so, why?

_____

_____

_____

Great Bible Stories: Hannah and Her Son

The Story:
Read 1 Samuel 1:1–27.

What did Hannah want more than anything in the world?

_____

_____

What did Hannah promise God?

_____

_____

How do you think Hannah felt when she brought Samuel to the temple and said goodbye to him, knowing he would never again live at home with her?

_____

_____

Hannah was a woman who knew what it meant to dream. Although she had a husband who loved her and a comfortable life, there was one thing that she wanted more than anything in the world—a child of her own. But Hannah also knew where to turn for the answer to her dream: she turned to God, and she trusted Him.

The thing that I think makes Hannah such a great example of surrender is what she prayed when she asked God for what she wanted. A lot of the time we are afraid to ask God for what we want. The problem with our prayers is not that we ask, or even what we ask for, but how we ask. Hannah is a great example of how to ask: even in praying for what she wants, she's already surrendering her desire to God. "Lord," she prays, "If You will only give me a son, then I will give him to You." Her motive in asking is a good one: she wants to have a son so that she can offer him to the Lord, and he can spend his life serving the Lord.

The best part of the story occurs after Hannah prays. In verse 18, the Bible tells us, "When she left and ate something, she was not sad anymore." In other words, she went away happy! Even though God hadn't yet answered her prayer, she was already comforted because she trusted God. She put her dream in His hands, knowing that no matter what He decided, everything would turn out for the good. That's what it means to surrender—to believe with all your heart that God will take care of you, and your dreams.

Why is it so hard to sometimes trust God?

_____

_____

_____

_____

_____

Look up Jeremiah 29:11–13. Write these verses down here.

_____

_____

_____

_____

_____

_____

Activity:
Understanding Surrender

Surrender is . . .

Circle the three words or phrases that best explain what surrender means to you:

giving up

letting go

forgetting

losing

trusting

hoping

Write your own definition of surrender:

_____
_____
_____
_____
_____
_____

Remember the Good Things

There's a saying: "Whatever God takes away with His left hand, He gives back with His right." The story of Hannah is a great example of this; although she gave her firstborn son to God, she was later blessed with three more sons and two daughters—and remember—she was barren for years before Samuel was born!

All through the Bible, God encourages us to remember the good things He has done for us in the past (read 1 Chronicles 16:12). When we remember the ways God has blessed our obedience to Him in the past, it makes it easier for us to let go of the things we want and give them to Him whole-heartedly.

Use this space to remember good things God has done for you!

What I have been afraid to ask, but truly want to pray for is . . .

_____

_____

_____

In the past, I have surrendered to God by . . .

_____

_____

_____

God blessed me by . . .

_____

_____

_____

_____

_____

_____

LESSON 3

Watching Your Eyes

Reflect

If the eyes are "windows to the soul," then we should be very careful what we allow to gain entry into our minds through them.

When you're lying in bed just about to fall asleep, what do you usually think about?

_____

_____

_____

What's the first thing you think about when you wake up in the morning?

_____

_____

_____

_____

Thoughts

After a long day spent at an adventure park have you ever then lain in bed and had the feeling that you were still riding a roller coaster? Sometimes the sensation of movement is so realistic that you think you'll fall right out of the bed. Since I only rarely go to adventure parks, the feeling of falling out of my bed is not one that I experience often. However, I think the fact that

15

it happens at all tells us our brains store information that can come out in our thoughts later.

Whatever we constantly put into our minds by the things we look at, listen to, read, and think about, is exactly what will ultimately come out of our minds.

There's an acronym that's often used among computer programmers: GIGO. It stands for Garbage In, Garbage Out. Anyone who works with computers knows: if the answer comes out wrong, it means that some information was put in wrong. What you put into a computer is exactly what you will get out of it. And although our brains are far more complex and complicated than any computer, this is one characteristic that they have in common.

"Selfish people are always worrying about how much the food costs. They tell you, 'Eat and drink,' but they don't really mean it."

—PROVERBS 23:7 NCV

What we read, listen to, and experience—the things we do—become the things we think. And the Bible tells us that what we think ultimately becomes what we are. Wow! That's frightening—the things you put into your mind will ultimately become what you are. Just like the saying, "You are what you eat," you could almost say that, in the long run, "You are what you see and hear."

What are three things that you like to do in your free time?

_____

_____

_____

_____

What were the last three movies you saw? The last two books you read? The last CD you bought? How does their content affect you?

_____

_____

_____

_____

The answers to those questions tell you a lot about yourself. What kinds of things do you choose to experience, read, or view in your free time, for your own entertainment? Of course there are as many different tastes in hobbies and activities as there are people in the world, and there's no implication here that certain genres of music or types of activities are better or worse. But there are positive choices to suit almost every taste—in music, for example, there are Christian bands of every genre imaginable. But if you enjoy constantly listening to, reading, or watching things that glorify violence, negativity, cruelty, and sex—or even make light of unkindness, intolerance, gossip, and backbiting—how long do you think it will take before those things start to show themselves in your own life—first in your thoughts, and ultimately in your actions?

Look again at your list of recent activities, and ask yourself: Do these things represent the kind of person I want to be?

_____

_____

_____

Great Love Stories: David and Bathsheeba

The Story:
Read 2 Samuel 11:1–27.

This passage gives us a glimpse into the power of temptation to seduce even the most faithful and godly of people. Throughout his life, David demonstrates character of the highest level. He is the innocent shepherd boy who writes hundreds of praise songs, the young man who fearlessly faces down a giant, the unlikely youngest son who is chosen to be king, and the powerful soldier who leads Israel bravely in battle against her enemies. In his relationship with Saul—the previous king of Israel—he shows an amazing respect for God's timing and authority as he refuses to make himself king, waiting instead for God to fulfill His promise.

And yet, even David was not exempt from the powerful temptation of the eyes, and this passage shows how even he could succumb in an instant. But although the whole thing happened so quickly, this story also demonstrates

17

although the whole thing happened so quickly, this story also demonstrates that temptation usually comes in stages, with plenty of "red flags" along the way to warn you that you're moving down a dangerous path. There are several moments in the story when David could have prevented the whole thing from happening. Recognizing those "red flags" is one of the key steps to preventing a fall into temptation.

In this passage, what was David's first mistake?

_____

_____

_____

_____

_____

What actions could David have changed to stop his slide into temptation?

_____

_____

_____

_____

In just one evening, David went from admiring a married woman in the distance to getting her pregnant. And his further actions demonstrate the swift downslide of sin—having committed adultery, he quickly went from manipulation and lying to murder, in order to cover it up.

If you read further in the story, you'll see that David eventually repented, and God forgave him willingly. However, there are serious consequences to his sin. Not only does the son who is born to Bathsheeba die (2 Sam. 12:14), but David's "small" sin had far-reaching consequences that extended to his entire family and even the next generation (2 Sam. 12:10). And the record of this instance—the one blemish on David's life of faith, praise, courage, and obedience—stands forever as a warning to the danger of looking at something we shouldn't.

"Brothers and sisters, think about the things that are good and worthy of praise. Think about the things that are true and honorable and right and pure and beautiful and respected."

—PHILIPPIANS 4:8 NCV

Our culture is full of negative things to fill our minds with. However, God has also filled the world with many beautiful and positive things to look at and think about! Use this list as a beginning point, and add your own ideas for ways to fill your mind with encouraging thoughts and positive images.

Stars and mountains
Faces of friends
My family around the kitchen table
A friend or relative's sports team
Good movies (list your favorites!)
Good books (list your favorite authors)
Kids playing

Cloud pictures
Famous paintings
Historical buildings
The Bible
Christian radio or CDs
Classical concerts

God, I confess the negative things I have put into my mind by . . .

From now on, my standards for what I put into my mind will be . . .

LESSON 4

Avoiding Evil

Reflect

It's compromise in little areas that often leads to bad decisions later. It's strength and courage shown in the "small" tests of life that make the "big" decisions easy.

How many of your friends outside of church know that you're a Christian?

_____

_____

_____

_____

How do people know what you believe?

_____

_____

_____

_____

Thoughts

Just for a minute, imagine that it is illegal to be a Christian. You, along with all the members of your church, are arrested and thrown in jail.

The day of your trial comes, and you are brought into the courtroom. You sit helplessly, forbidden to speak, and watch as a series of witnesses—your friends, neighbors, and even relatives—are forced to testify against you. They are asked numerous questions about your life and activities, everything they observed in your life. The prosecuting attorney tries to prove that you are indeed a Christian and should be put back in jail for life.

Would there be enough evidence to convict you?

Yes, it's an extreme and improbable situation. But the question remains: if someone were to look at your life, not just what you say but how you live, not just in church but all the time, how obvious would your faith be? It's said that "actions speak louder than words," and words are often the least convincing aspect of our lives.

"Do not hold back the work of the Holy Spirit. Do not treat prophecy as if it were unimportant. But test everything. Keep what is good, and stay away from everything that is evil."

—1 THESSALONIANS 5:19–22 NCV

Sometimes, what we don't do is even more powerful than what we do. Maybe you go to church and youth group—but a lot of people do that. Maybe you go to small group or a Bible study; maybe you even pray and read the Bible regularly on your own—but most people don't see that. What about the part of your life that is on display, every day, all the time? What about your daily interactions with people, the daily "small" temptations you face, the potentially compromising situations that seem insignificant or even petty? It's in those situations that what you do can really make you stand out from the crowd. Sure, people might make fun of you or criticize you if you take a stand on issues that seem absurd to them, like practicing abstinence or refraining from watching R-rated movies. But, they will take notice. And if people know that you take a stand on those issues because of your faith, a lot of times they can't help but respect you—even if they disagree with you.

When have you taken a stand because of a personal conviction? How did people react?

_____

_____

_____

What areas in your life are potentially compromising and where you have not set a standard for yourself?

_____

_____

_____

One of the great advantages of setting a high standard for yourself in seemingly unimportant areas is that it makes it much easier for you to make good decisions when big temptations come along. In fact, if you are careful to identify and avoid situations that are compromising, then many times the big temptation won't come along, ever. You'll be able to "head temptation off at the pass," preventing it from attacking you before it even gets close. If you set a standard that you're not going to be sexually involved with a man, then it's highly unlikely that you'll find yourself in a situation where you're tempted to have sex. Or if you decide that you're never going to try even one drink, then you'll never be in much danger of becoming an alcoholic.

Pray for what standards you should set in those areas of potential compromise. And when you do set standards, think about not only the effect your actions have on you, but also how they could look to other people. People watch you more than you think, and what you do—even what you seem to do—can affect what they think about you and what they believe about your faith.

Great Bible Stories: Daniel and the Diet

The Scene:

Jerusalem, God's chosen city, fell to its enemies. The heathen king of Babylonia took the city captive, and many of the Israelites were captured and made into servants for the pagan king. Daniel was one of the captives.

In the Old Testament, God told His people to set themselves apart from the nations around them by the way they lived—to make it obvious by how they dressed, what they ate, and what they did that they were different from the nations around them. One of the main customs adopted to demonstrate their faith was their diet; God gave them a list of "kosher" foods—items acceptable to eat. But the king of Babylon didn't care about the Israelites' dietary scruples, and he wanted his servants well nourished and healthy. So the captured Israelites were offered a menu dictated by the royal palace. Many of the foods were non-kosher—foods that God had forbidden to His chosen people. And although he was a prisoner in a foreign land, Daniel was determined to continue to represent God even in the smallest details in the way he lived.

The Story:
Read Daniel 1:1–16.

What plan did Daniel form to persuade the guard to let him change his diet?

_____

_____

_____

_____

_____

What was the result of his experiment?

_____

_____

_____

_____

One thing I love about Daniel is that his story makes it clear that you don't have to be an eccentric or a "weirdo" to uphold high standards of purity. There were a lot of ways Daniel could have handled this situation. He could have just gone on a fast and refused to eat anything until they brought him something kosher. If he'd done that, he probably would have just been killed—or left to starve—and we never would have heard his story. Or he could have just eaten the food he was offered, reasoned that God would overlook the fact that it wasn't really kosher since he was a captive in a foreign country and didn't have a choice about what he ate. But Daniel came up with a third solution, one in which he was able to hold fast to his standards without offending the guard who was in authority over him. He suggested an experiment: a ten-day vegetable-only diet. Then he trusted the results to God. It doesn't say so in this passage, but from what we learn about Daniel in the rest of the stories, he spent a lot of time praying he'd be healthy enough to continue the diet. And God answered beyond his expectations—not only was Daniel allowed to stay with kosher foods, but all the other captives were switched to the same food! A surprising twist, an unbelieving guard then forced all of Daniel's peers to live according to the standard of purity and obedience that Daniel had set.

In the same way, we can be pure without being offensive. If we set an example in a way that is appropriate and encouraging, not only will it affect our lives positively, it can influence and inspire everyone around us.

What would you have done in Daniel's situation?

_____
_____
_____
_____
_____
_____

Have you ever given in on one of your standards because of outside pressure?

_____
_____
_____
_____

Have you ever offended someone who wasn't a believer because you held a personal conviction in a way that was confrontational and judgmental? Think about it.

_____
_____
_____
_____

Quiz:
How Would This Look to You?

Take a look at your life from an outsider's perspective! If you really want to be an example in the world, you have to think about not only what you're really doing but also how it will look to those who observe you. What would you think if you saw someone you knew (or *thought* you knew) was a Christian in the following situations? Maybe it's innocent—but be honest with yourself: how does it look? How can you be a witness without being judgmental in the "grey areas"? What would you do in these situations?

1. A friend who lives on your hall says that she's a Christian. This morning on your way to an 8:00 A.M. class, you saw a guy in a t-shirt and boxers coming out of her room. You're pretty sure he didn't stop by for a quick visit this early in the day! But you've met the guy before, and your friend assured you they are "just friends." You:

    a. Don't do anything—it's none of your business.

    b. Mention it in passing to your friend next time you see her, to find out if she wants to talk about it.

    c. Sit your friend down for a serious talk at the first opportunity; it may be okay, but if you care about her and her witness as a Christian, it's your responsibility to hold her accountable.

    d. Reprimand the guy then and there—he's clearly a serious temptation problem for your friend.

    e. Buy a copy of *Wait for Me* for your friend; obviously she isn't really a Christian, so it's time to start witnessing to her!

2. You see a friend from your Bible study group hanging out in the alley behind the gym—along with all the smokers. You don't see a cigarette in his hand, but there's so much smoke around him that it's hard to tell! You:

    a. Walk right over there and ask him what he's doing with people who are obviously the "wrong crowd."

    b. Catch him later in science class and ask what was going on.

c. Join him and start talking about Bible study—this is a great opportunity to share your faith with the school druggies.

d. Say a prayer for him on your way to your next class.

3. You're walking into math class, hoping nervously that you're ready for the test you're about to take. Near the doorway, you see a group of students from your class gathered around a guy who you know is in the same math class during the previous hour. He's showing them a paper that, even at a distance, looks suspiciously like a copy of the test. One of the people in the group is a friend of yours from your accountability group at church. You:

a. Walk into class and tell the teacher you think they might be cheating.

b. Go straight to your desk and try to concentrate on some last minute studying—you have your own grade to worry about!

c. Confront the group and ask them what they're doing.

d. Join the group—if they have answers to the test questions, your grade in this class could really use a boost, and if your friend from church is doing it, too, then it must be okay.

e. Go to your desk and secretly pass an anonymous note to the teacher, telling her there's something in the hall that she should investigate.

4. It's Friday afternoon, and everybody is going to the big party tonight. You're invited, but you're pretty sure that everyone will be getting drunk, and you're not sure you want to be a part of that scene. But all of your friends are going—especially one friend who tells you she really wants to continue the conversation you've been having with her about your faith. You:

a. Go to the party with your friend—sure, it's not the best environment for a serious conversation, but you want to meet her where she's at.

b. Call a couple of friends from church and invite them to come with you, so at least you'll know that not *everyone* will be drinking, and maybe they can help you answer your friend's questions about faith.

c. Talk your friend into coming with you to check out the new Starbucks® that just opened instead—and she can go to the party later if she wants, but without you.

Because I want to avoid even a hint of evil in any aspect of my life, I commit myself to the following standards:

Regarding friendships with men:

Regarding dating relationships:

Regarding food, drink, clothes, and entertainment:

Regarding places I go:

Setting Your Limits

Reflect

Someone who is trying to please God shouldn't be asking how close to the edge she can go before crossing the line. A Christian woman should be more concerned with how close she can get to God.

How good are you at accomplishing the goals you set for yourself?

_____
_____
_____

What about keeping the limits you set for yourself?

_____
_____
_____

Thoughts

It's probably the most common question asked about the issue of physical intimacy: how far is too far? How much can you do with your date before you're officially sinning? Many teens wonder exactly at what point do you cross the line?

The Bible isn't squeamish about giving us specific instructions on taboo topics. In the Old Testament, God gave the Israelites instructions related to all sorts of physical and sexual issues. However, on the issue of levels of physical intimacy before marriage, the Bible is strangely silent. Scripture is very clear that sex outside of marriage is not God's plan for us, but it says nothing about kissing, hugging, "making out," or all the different levels of intimacy that lead up to the act of sex. The specifics of "how far is too far" is left entirely up to us to discern. This is a problem because . . .

_____

_____

_____

_____

It might be easier to resist sexual temptation if God gave us a clear command on this issue. Because sexual activity is designed to accelerate, the farther you go, the harder is it to stop. But I believe that God left this topic unanswered for a reason. The truth is that asking how far we can go sexually is the wrong question for us to be asking in the first place.

What reasons can you think of for having some level of physical affection in a dating relationship?

_____

_____

_____

In a godly relationship, what would be the purpose of physical affection?

_____

_____

_____

Much more than what we do with our bodies, God is concerned about what's going on inside our hearts and our minds. It's possible to be "pure" physically while being lustful, selfish, and adulterous in your thoughts. If your biggest concern is how far you can go and still be "okay," then that's a sign of something off center in your way of thinking and in your heart.

Ask yourself: Is the level of affection in your relationship helping you to experience God's love, or is it encouraging lust? To flesh out these hard answers, continue to break it down by asking: Where are you trying to go with this relationship, and especially with the physical part of it? Where will each action lead you, and what are the consequences? This process will help you decide where to set limits regarding sexual intimacy.

How else can you discern for yourself how far is too far, and set healthy limits?

_____

_____

_____

_____

"So brothers and sisters, since God has shown us great mercy, I beg you to offer your lives as a living sacrifice to him. Your offering must be only for God and pleasing to him, which is the spiritual way for you to worship. Do not change yourselves to be like the people of this world, but be changed within by a new way of thinking. Then you will be able to decide what God wants for you; you will know what is good and pleasing to him and what is perfect."

—ROMANS 12:1, 2 NCV

Although this passage isn't talking specifically about sex, it could have been written in answer to the question of how far is okay. With a little interpretation, it gives us practical advice for making decisions on where to set those limits on physical intimacy. First, this passage tells us to offer our bodies to God as "living sacrifices." This is a paradox because in the Old Testament, a sacrifice was something—usually an animal—that was killed and offered to God on the altar. But God tells us that we are *living sacrifices* which means while we are on this earth, we are to offer our physical bodies to God for His purpose. By offering your body to God, you set your primary motivations with experiencing God. So if we truly offer our bodies as sacrifices to God, that action means from that moment on, everything we do with our physical bodies should be to please Him, to honor Him, and most of all to fulfill His purpose in our lives.

In addition, this passage says that the things we do physically are a "spiritual way for you to worship." It's easy to forget that everything we do 24/7 has a spiritual impact. Sometimes we compartmentalize our lives and reserve our relationship with God for Sunday mornings and in our quiet times, but tell ourselves that Saturday night only affects us. The truth is that God says that what He wants from us is not just our spiritual worship but our physical obedience—that is the worship that truly pleases Him.

Great Love Stories: Joseph and Mary

The Scene:
Read Matthew 1:18–25.

Why was Joseph considering divorcing Mary?

_____

_____

_____

_____

Why do you think Joseph "had no union" with Mary even after they were married until Jesus had been born?

_____

_____

_____

_____

In Joseph and Mary's time, just like today, it wasn't uncommon for engaged couples to begin having sex before they were married. After all, you're going to be married anyway, right? Many people argue that once a relationship has the definite commitment of engagement, then it's okay to have sex. But Joseph and Mary evidently didn't think so, even though an engagement in those days was much more binding than it is today—so much so that in order to break it off, you actually had to obtain a legal divorce.

Although they were practically married, we know that Joseph and Mary were not having sex because when he found out Mary was pregnant, Joseph knew it was not his because they had not consummated their union yet. He then seriously considered breaking off their engagement as he assumed, naturally enough, that she cheated on him. It took an angel's announcement to convince Joseph to stay with Mary and avoid the scandal of an illegitimate birth—and out of great respect, Matthew tells us that Joseph "had no relations" with Mary until after the birth of Jesus. Joseph and Mary waited until after Jesus was born to have sex. That is admirable self-control! I mean, they were married, and they were both virgins; they'd been waiting long enough, and everything was perfect, right? But Joseph chose to abstain from having sex with his wife until after Jesus had been born. By law, Joseph had every right to be with her, but out of respect for the miracle that God was doing in her, he chose to wait. Or, perhaps the idea of having sex with Mary while the son of God was still in her womb was a pretty overwhelming thought.

But although Mary is the only person who will ever bear the son of God in her womb, Paul says to us that "Your bodies are parts of Christ himself" (1 Cor. 6:15, NCV). If you have given your heart in trust to Jesus and asked for salvation, then He promises that He will send the Holy Spirit to live inside you. Paul uses this truth to argue against sexual immorality.

"Surely you know that your bodies are parts of Christ himself. So I must never take the parts of Christ and join them to a prostitute! It is written in the Scriptures, 'The two will become one body.' So you should know that anyone who joins with a prostitute becomes one body with the prostitute. But the one who joins with the Lord is one spirit with the Lord.

So run away from sexual sin. Every other sin people do is outside their bodies, but those who sin sexually sin against their own bodies. You should know that your body is a temple for the Holy Spirit who is in you. You have received the Holy Spirit from God. So you do not belong to yourselves, because you were bought by God for a price. So honor God with your bodies."

—1 CORINTHIANS 6:15–20 NCV

What level of physical intimacy in a dating relationship do you believe would be most honoring to God?

_____
_____
_____
_____

How far is too far when you consider that your body is a temple of the Holy Spirit?

_____

_____

_____

_____

_____

_____

_____

_____

Amazing as it is, Paul implies in this passage that what a Christian does with his body, Christ is also doing. Since Christ lives in us, whatever we do with our bodies we also force Him to do. If that truth becomes your guideline, then it becomes much easier to define your limits!

Choosing Your Limits

It's great to understand the idea of the importance of purity, but if you don't make clear and specific commitments about your physical limits, then your chances of maintaining purity are slim. The time to choose where you'll set your limits is not when you're out on a great date and caught up in passionate emotions (or hormones). Long before that, you have to make up your mind exactly which expressions of affection are pure and which are not. You have to know where your limits are before you ever get in the situation. Then, should you ever get close to "crossing the line," you won't be as overwhelmed by passion—you'll know that you're close to doing something you already decided was wrong.

In reflecting on this issue, a lot of women tend to think that anything they've done already is "okay" and anything else is "too far." But be careful! Especially if you're more experienced, you might have to set more conservative limits in order to avoid falling into temptation. Physical activity in a relationship always tends to escalate. If things get too far too fast, it becomes much harder to "put on the brakes." Set limits where you'll be able to stop immediately if things get close to crossing them.

Knowing that my body is the temple of the Holy Spirit and that anything I do, Christ is also doing, I believe that the following expressions of affection are appropriate and pure in a dating relationship:

_____

_____

_____

_____

Right now, I make a commitment to not go beyond the following limitations of physical intimacy until I am married:

_____

_____

_____

_____

Confessions

Lord Jesus, I want to confess to You the ways that I have crossed these limits, either physically or mentally, by . . .

_____

_____

_____

_____

Thank You for forgiving me.

_____

_____

_____

_____

From now on, please help me to live to Your standards by . . .

_____

_____

_____

_____

Amen.

LESSON 6

Facing the Consequences

Reflect

Emotional and spiritual pain will affect your walk with Christ, the spiritual intimacy you are meant to enjoy with your future spouse, and the way you view yourself. God wants you to be healthy—physically, emotionally, and spiritually.

What are the worst consequences you have ever experienced from a mistake?

_____

_____

_____

"So run away from sexual sin. Every other sin people do is outside their bodies, but those who sin sexually sin against their own bodies."

—1 CORINTHIANS 6:18 NCV

Thoughts

Think about your body for a minute. Sure, we all have things we don't like about our bodies, and we all have times when we don't take care of our bodies the way we should. But can you imagine, for example, deliberately going for three weeks without a shower? Or going for weeks without eating? Or deliberately causing yourself pain? Generally, any of these actions would be a serious sign of unhealthiness. A healthy woman is one who automatically takes care of her body.

Perhaps you've read in the Bible about the disease, leprosy. It's a disease easily preventable by good hygiene and the use of vaccines, and in developed countries, leprosy has nearly completely disappeared. However, in Third World countries, where hygiene is often poor and vaccines unavailable, this is a disease that remains a very real threat to millions of people.

Although leprosy is usually eventually fatal, leprosy itself does not kill you. It only affects the nerves in the skin—deadening them and destroying them until the sick person is unable to feel anything. Sufferers of leprosy are unable to feel the pain that warns a healthy person that something is wrong with their body, and so they suffer from numerous other injuries without realizing it. A leper could stand with his hand in a fire and not feel it burning; he could catch his fingers in a door and leave his finger behind without even knowing it was missing. Because of accidents such as this, lepers are often easily recognizable by the disfigurements and scars that mark them.

And although we rarely see leprosy in the developed world today, I believe that our culture suffers from an epidemic of spiritual leprosy. In matters related to sex, we are so saturated with objectifying images and peer pressure to act on base emotion, so surrounded by lies concealing what true intimacy is that our consciences are deadened to the dangers of sexual sin. We are like lepers who can't feel the warning symptoms of spiritual pain. In spite of the evidence all around us, we simply can't see the deadly consequences of our actions until it is too late. We can stand with our hands deep in the fire of passion and not even feel that we're being burned. I don't want to be a "doomsayer," but I think it is essential that we remind ourselves of the dangers of sexual sin. They are much greater and more lasting than we frequently realize.

What do you think are the greatest dangers of sex outside of marriage?

_____

_____

_____

For you, what would be the worst possible consequence of having sex?

_____

_____

_____

The most common answers to that question are probably pregnancy and STDs. Both of those are terrible and difficult consequences, often with life-long physical effects. It is important that we realize the powerful emotional and spiritual consequences that sex has on our lives. Just one sexual act can have consequences that affect us, our friends, our families, our future spouses, and our children for years to come.

Great Bible Stories: Abram's Impatience

The Scene:
Read Genesis 15:1–6; 16:1–15.

What did God promise Abram (later known as Abraham)?

_____

_____

_____

Why did it seem unlikely that God's promise would be fulfilled?

_____

_____

_____

In Abram's day, having lots of children was a symbol not only of riches and success but also of God's blessing. A woman without children was considered cursed by God. And so it was a common practice for women who were barren to have children through their servants. If a woman's husband slept with her servant, the servant's children would actually be considered part of the wife's family.

However, as we see in Sarai's (later known as Sarah) story, the plan could easily backfire. Although custom considered Hagar's son legitimate, God intended to give Abram and Sarai children of their own, through their marriage relationship. And even though having her servant Hagar sleep with her husband was actually Sarai's idea, she discovered after they'd done it that she wasn't really happy with the result. Even though the relationship between Abram and Hagar was considered acceptable in the culture of their day, it was a far cry from God's plan for Abram's family.

Why do you think Sarai suggested that her husband sleep with another woman? Why would Abram have agreed to it?

_____

_____

_____

_____

Although God had clearly promised Abram a son, neither Abram nor Sarai was willing to wait for God's timing. They took matters into their own hands, perhaps thinking that "God helps those who help themselves" and feeling that God could use a hand in fulfilling His promise. God didn't punish Abram for this lack of faith, and He even said that He would bless Hagar's son, Ishmael. However, there were still several significant consequences to this seemingly insignificant sin.

What were the consequences to Abram's sleeping with Hagar?

_____

_____

_____

_____

_____

In addition to the conflict that developed in their own home—between Sarai and Hagar, and then between Sarai and Abram—as a result of this sin, there were far-reaching consequences. The descendents of Hagar's son Ishmael eventually became the Arabic peoples, and even today we can see the conflict between them and the descendents of Isaac, the son that Sarai and Abram later had, in the war between Palestinians and Israelites in the Middle East. This seemingly innocent and inconsequential sin had results that we can still see in the world today, thousands of years later! You can never know how far-reaching the consequences of your sin might be. The greater the calling that God has chosen for your life, the greater the influence that He wants you to have on the world, the greater the consequences of your sin could become. Even your smallest decisions to compromise could have a powerful ripple effect on your life and the lives of others in thousands of ways you can't even imagine.

My Motivations

It's important for you to obey God's commands and stay pure in every area of your life, especially when it comes to sex. What motivates you to follow God in your dating relationships? As you reflect on the reasons why it's important to wait, you'll strengthen your resolve and commitment to purity. Use these ideas as a beginning point, and create your own list of reasons why it's best to wait. Keep this list as a reminder when you're tempted to help you remember the importance of purity in your own life.

My reasons for waiting:

- the dangers of sex

- my love for my husband

- the consequences in my family

- the consequences to my Christian witness

- others . . .

_____

_____

_____

_____

_____

_____

_____

_____

_____

_____

God's Forgiveness

It may be that you have already experienced the terrible consequences of sex outside of marriage. Or maybe you haven't actually had sex, but you've gone farther physically than you believe God wanted you to. The beauty of our God is that He always stands ready and willing to forgive us. In the last chapter, you wrote a confession of ways that you have crossed the limits of God's standards for you. Now, take a few minutes to reflect on God's forgiveness.

Lord, I know that You have forgiven me because . . .
(Write out passages of scripture that promise His forgiveness. If you can't find any, ask a parent, youth pastor, or Bible study leader to help you.)

God, Your forgiveness makes me feel . . .

I thank You because . . .

Amen.

Becoming "the One"

Reflect

Don't pine about the house waiting for your prince to come along! God made this world, this life, for us to enjoy, and subsequently praise Him for.

Describe your personality in three words.

_____

_____

_____

What are your best character traits?

_____

_____

_____

What are your worst faults?

_____

_____

_____

Thoughts

It's easy for women to dream about what they are looking for in a relationship with a man. I think most of us girls have imagined that God will someday give us a husband who will be godly, fun, interesting, smart, and pretty much perfect in every way! But while it's easy to focus on what you want in a relationship, it's much harder to focus on who you need to be in order to be the right person for such a relationship. If you want to marry a great, godly person, the first step is to for you to become a great, godly person.

However, if your own spiritual growth is centered around the great relationship that God might give you someday, then you'll never really be able to focus on all the things that God has for you right now in this stage of your life. God doesn't want us to spend our time sitting around waiting, wishing, and hoping for the future. Yes, He wants us to anticipate it, but the most important thing is for us to see what God is doing right now in our lives, to learn the lessons He's teaching us today and enjoy the blessings He's giving us. If all of your hopes are focused around the future, you'll miss out on everything God has for you today.

> *"The LORD's love never ends; his mercies never stop. They are new every morning; LORD, your loyalty is great. I say to myself, 'The LORD is mine, so I hope in him.'"*
>
> —LAMENTATIONS 3:22–24 NCV

God's goodness, His purpose, and His love for us is "new every morning"—it's never caught up in the past or the future. God has a plan for your life—not just for your entire life overall, but for every day and even every minute of your life. Every morning when you wake up, He has a way for you to serve Him that day, a way for you to enjoy Him, a way for you to love His people and experience His presence. If you spend all your time caught up in regretting the past or wondering about the future, you'll miss out on the plans He has for you today.

So much of our culture is focused on self-realization. We are flooded with self-help books, self-focused meditation and groups, and hundreds of methods to discover our "true selves." But finding your true self isn't just about knowing who you are; it's about discovering who God intended for you to be when He made you. Becoming the right person for the relationship God has planned for you someday isn't something you can do by sitting around waiting for it to come along or by constantly searching for the person for you to be with. You can only grow into the person God made you to be by living in the present, by learning every day to know God better and searching every day for the ways He has provided you to love Him that day.

When was the last time you went out of your way to serve someone else?

_____

_____

_____

_____

Who was the last person you prayed for?

_____

_____

_____

_____

Which do you spend more time doing—asking God for things or thanking Him for what He's given you?

_____

_____

_____

_____

Telling, isn't it? Where is the focus of your life, really? If you're focused on the blessings you hope that God will someday give you in the future, then not only will you miss out on what He's giving you now—you'll also never become the kind of person you need to be in order to receive the blessings of the future. But if you're focused on the blessings, the friendships, and the opportunities to serve others and know Him that He's giving you every day, then not only will you enjoy life to the fullest now—you'll also be preparing yourself for the relationship He might have planned for you.

Great Love Stories: Boaz and Ruth

The Scene:
Read Ruth 1—4.

In chapter 1, what does Ruth tell Naomi? Why do you think she chose to stay with her mother-in-law after her husband was dead?

_____

_____

_____

What could Ruth have gained by going home? What could she hope to gain by staying with Naomi?

_____

_____

_____

Ruth 1:16, 17 is one of the most beautiful passages of loyalty in the entire Bible. I've often seen this verse quoted at weddings as a picture of the loyalty and devotion between a husband and wife. However, when it was first spoken, these words were not describing love between a husband and wife but rather between a daughter and her mother-in-law.

Naomi, her husband, and their two sons were Israelites who had come to live in the country of Moab. Ruth married one of Naomi's sons, but unfortunately, he died. At that point, Ruth didn't have any remaining obligations to stay with or help Naomi. She was free to go back to her own home, to her own parents, and perhaps find another husband from her own people. Why instead did she choose to accompany Naomi to a foreign land? The Bible doesn't tell us everything that was going on in Ruth's heart, but it's clear that she had grown to love her mother-in-law dearly, and she had also grown to love the God of her new family. "Your people will be my people," she tells Naomi, "and your God will be my God" (1:16). Ruth isn't looking for a new life or a new husband; she isn't focused on herself at all. Instead, she is focused on serving and taking care of her mother-in-law. Naomi was old, and she'd been away from her homeland for many years. Ruth knew that it was possible that many of Naomi's old relatives and friends would no longer be alive; they certainly wouldn't be anticipating her return. Naomi would need someone to help her as she restarted her life, and although Ruth was still a young woman who could hope to marry again, she was happy to give up her own prospects for the future in order to take care of her mother-in-law.

How does Boaz meet Ruth?

_____

_____

_____

What does Boaz say about Ruth when he first meets her?

_____

_____

What kind of woman is Ruth?

_____

_____

Boaz and Ruth first meet when Ruth is gleaning in his fields. The practice of gleaning was a provision in the laws of Israel that was meant to take care of the poor. Anyone who was too poor to own their own fields or buy their own grain was allowed to go to the wheat fields of a stranger and harvest behind the harvesters, gathering the leftovers for themselves. By law, land owners were required to leave some grain—the "gleanings"—for the poor. However, gleaning could be dangerous work, especially for a woman alone. Just as in any culture, men who worked in the fields could be a rough sort. And gathering grain was long, sweaty work. It was these dangers that Ruth had wanted to spare her elderly mother-in-law. So she took it upon herself to go alone to the fields, although she was a stranger and a foreigner there. She basically went to the first field she found and worked as hard as she could. But in God's providence, the first field she came to just happened to belong to Boaz—a relative of Naomi's.

Boaz was impressed with Ruth from the moment he saw her. Perhaps he noticed her simply because he didn't recognize her, and he wondered who the foreigner was. The Bible doesn't mention whether she was beautiful; it doesn't say that Boaz was impressed with her looks. Even if she was beautiful, she probably wasn't looking her best after hours of working out in the sun. But Boaz was impressed with her character. Although she'd only been in Israel a short time, she had already acquired a reputation as a godly woman. "I know about all the help you have given your mother-in-law," Boaz says to her (Ruth 2:11, NCV). He has heard about her servant heart and her courage, and that is much more impressive to him than surface beauty. He notices Ruth because of the kind of person that she is.

In the rest of the story, we learn that Boaz is not just a relative of Naomi's but actually a "kinsman-redeemer." In the laws of Israel in those days, if a man died without children, his closest surviving relative was expected to marry his widow in order to continue the dead man's family line. After having heard and observed what a godly woman Ruth was, Boaz was happy to marry her—not just for custom but for love. And not only did Ruth gain a godly husband and later a son, but God chose this couple to be ancestors of the royal line of Israel. Ruth, an unknown foreigner, became the great-grandmother of King David and an ancestor of Jesus Himself.

If a stranger were to ask your friends about you, what would they say?

_____
_____
_____
_____
_____
_____

Ruth's reputation was the most impressive thing about her. She built a reputation not on making herself beautiful or seeking romantic relationships but on serving those closest to her and seeking God, even when it meant sacrifices for herself. She was truly a woman who was worthy of true love, but she didn't make that her first priority. Instead, her priority was to serve those who needed her most, and God provided her with a relationship that was better than anything she could have found for herself.

Quiz:
Are you ready for true love?

Before you can find "the one," you need to *be* "the one." How close are you? If God were to bring the perfect future spouse into your life right now, would they even be attracted to you? Are you the kind of person who would attract a godly man or woman? Take this quiz to find out!

1. What kinds of things do you usually pray for?

    a. A romantic relationship is the number one thing on your list!

    b. God is like Santa—you spend all your prayer time telling Him your list.

    c. You mostly thank Him for things He's done for you.

    d. You don't pray much.

2. How often do you read the Bible?

    a. Once a week, in church

    b. Twice a week, in church and at youth group

    c. Every once in a while on your own

    d. You don't have a Bible.

3. How do you feel about church?

    a. You go only when your parents make you.

    b. You enjoy hanging out with your church friends.

    c. You're there every time they open the doors—when your parents want to punish you, they ground you from youth group.

Living in the Present

God, thank You for all the blessings You have given me today by . . .

Thank You for the opportunities You have given me today by . . .

Help me to be content with my life right now by . . .

Help me to serve and love You today by . . .

Amen.

LESSON 8

Being Single

Reflect

Whether God has called us to be married or single, it really comes down to the same thing—making Him our first love, focusing our gaze on Him.

What is the best part about not being in a romantic relationship?

_____

_____

_____

What is the worst part?

_____

_____

_____

Thoughts

A big question that often runs through a single girl's mind including mine, is "What if I never get married?" I think the fear of never getting married, of never finding a man to love, is one of the biggest fears of many young, single women. Most people long to be in a relationship, to have the security and comfort of having someone. The thought that this might never happen is a scary one.

The Bible says that some believers are given the "gift of celibacy," the spiritual gift of being single for life. A lot of Christians are terrified that God might give them that "gift"! Some people say that if you feel a longing for a relationship, then it means that you definitely don't have the gift of celibacy. However, just because you want something—like a romantic relationship—is no guarantee that God will ever give it to you. Yes, He wants to fulfill our desires and satisfy our hearts, but sometimes the things we long for are not the things that are best for us. And although women tend to believe that they *need* a man to truly be fulfilled, many of the most godly people in the Bible and throughout history—including Jesus Himself!—were single. So, the desire for a relationship is no guarantee that you'll someday be in one. In fact, I believe that God gives *everyone* the gift of celibacy, at least for the period in your life when you are single. For some of us, He may eventually take that gift away when His time is right to place us in a relationship and marriage. For others, He may never take that gift away, and we'll be single for the rest of our lives. However, that doesn't mean that we have to be unfulfilled, unhappy, or somehow "less" than those who are married. Although it often doesn't feel like it, God does describe singleness not as a curse but as a gift—a blessing to be grateful for.

"I know that you can do all things and that no plan of yours can be ruined."
—PSALM 42:2 NCV

The key to being satisfied in your single life is learning to direct your longing for love and security toward God rather than to men. Although God will use other people—both friendships and family as well as romantic relationships—to help satisfy our longings and draw us to Himself, no one man will ever be able to meet all our needs or satisfy our hearts the way that God can. He knows us and loves us more than any other person ever could. He is the only one who can truly satisfy the desires of our hearts. And even if He does give you a wonderful marriage relationship someday, the only way that marriage will prosper is if you continue to make Him the focus of your life and continue to let your heart be satisfied first by Him, before you turn to your husband.

How can you learn to know God while you are single in ways that would be more difficult after you're married?

_____

_____

There are many opportunities to serve and ways to build your relationship with God that are ideally suited to singleness. Taking a retreat of solitude, for example, which is something I really enjoy, would be harder after marriage because I would have a duty to my husband to spend time with him. Other ways you can serve God while you're single are going on short-term missions trips, volunteering at your church or in your community, and building friendships with a variety of people. Enjoying friendships with members of the opposite sex also helps your life to feel "full" while your single. The time of your life when you're not in a relationship with a man is a unique opportunity because you have more free time at your disposal than you are likely to have after marriage. After marriage, you'll have to consider the needs and desires of your husband in every decision you make, and you'll have to devote the first part of your time, after God, to him. But when you're single, you can explore different opportunities for service and ministry without having to consider the needs of your spouse for your time and attention. It's an opportunity that you may never have again! But if God does call you to be single for the rest of your life, then there's no better way to devote your time and energy than by loving Him and serving His people in every way you can.

Great Bible Stories: Paul's Single Life

The Scene:
Read 1 Corinthians 7:25–35.

What reasons does Paul give why it's "better" to be unmarried?

_____

_____

Paul, the writer of 1 Corinthians, also wrote most of the New Testament. Although he started out persecuting the church, after his conversion he became the greatest missionary in the early church. Without him, the gospel would never have spread as quickly as it did in the early days of Christianity.

However, Paul experienced a great deal of persecution as he struggled to share the gospel with unreached parts of the world. He describes the trials he experienced in 2 Corinthians 11:21–29. He was repeatedly imprisoned, whipped, shipwrecked, stoned, endangered, and even left for dead. It's hard to even imagine the difficulties he experienced! If anyone deserved the comfort of a wife to come home to after all his difficult journeys, it was certainly Paul.

> *"Do we not have the right to bring a believing wife with us when we travel as do the other apostles and the Lord's brothers and Peter? Are Barnabas and I the only ones who must work to earn our living?"*
>
> —1 Corinthians 9:5, 6 NCV

Although he often talked about the advantages of being single, Paul also hints that he would have appreciated the comfort of being married. He says that he could have gotten married, that it wouldn't have been wrong, and he implies that he wouldn't have minded getting married even though he advises other believers that they'll be happier if they're single.

However, Paul felt the advantages of his singleness much more than he missed the possibility of a wife. Considering all the persecutions and difficulties he went through, it's hard to imagine how he could have accomplished as much for God and for the church if he had been married. Someone who is married has to consider the welfare of their spouse; if Paul had been married, how would his wife have been provided for when he was in prison or on his missionary journeys? If she had come with him, how would she have stood up to the challenges of weather, danger, and beatings that Paul experienced on a daily basis? He knew that the best way he could accomplish his calling to preach the gospel was by being single, and by having the freedom to focus completely on what God was telling him to do.

What if God intends for you to remain single for your entire life? What are some possible ways that you could use the freedom of being single to serve Him more effectively?

_____

_____

What is something you do for yourself, God, or others that you promise not to give up when you get married?

_____

_____

Famous Singles in History

Besides Paul and Jesus, there have been many people in the history of the church who never married and served God much more effectively because of it. What do you know about the following leaders of the faith? Write what you know about their accomplishments for God, or do some research to learn more about them.

Mother Teresa

_____

_____

Amy Carmichael

_____

_____

Rich Mullins

_____

_____

St. Francis of Assisi

_____

_____

David Brainerd

_____

_____

Corrie ten Boom

_____

_____

Dietrich Bonhoeffer

_____

_____

The Advantages of a Single Life

Lord, thank You for the gift of singleness that You have given me for this
stage of my life. I am grateful for it because . . .

_____

_____

_____

_____

_____

_____

I will use it to serve You by . . .

_____

_____

_____

_____

_____

I will seek to make You my first love by . . .

_____

_____

_____

_____

_____

Amen.

LESSON 9

Learning to Serve

Reflect

Your marriage will never be a happy one as long as you are just looking out for yourself. Over and over I have heard couples, including my own parents, say that their marriage only became great when they learned to give, love, and serve more than they sought to receive. This is a principle we can be practicing now because it is a life principle, not just one that applies to marriage. Whenever we choose to serve ourselves, selfishness—not to mention unhappiness—grows. But when we give our lives up completely to God, to love and serve Him and then others, joy reigns in our hearts.

What do you hope to gain from being married? What do you hope to give to your marriage?

_____

_____

What does unconditional love mean to you?

_____

_____

Thoughts

When we think about marriage, we tend to think about the benefits that it will bring us. We want the companionship, the comfort, and the security of a relationship that we can always count on. It's so easy to imagine that marriage will solve all our emotional problems and give us a life of happily ever after. But actually the opposite is often true. From all that I've heard from married couples, marriage does more to bring out our issues than to solve them, making us aware of our selfishness and our sin in ways that no other relationship ever will. Any woman who goes into a marriage expecting it to make her life easier is probably in for a painful awakening.

It's obvious from the destroyed relationships we all can see around us that marriage takes a lot more than passion to make it work. It takes a level of commitment that goes beyond the selfish mindset programmed into us by our culture. We need to stop thinking about how marriage—and even our other relationships—will benefit us and instead focus on how they can teach us to serve. After all, the purpose of marriage is not really for us. God didn't invent marriage to make us more comfortable with our lives. He created it as an illustration of His love for us through His Son. His love requires absolute commitment on our part, to the point of taking up our cross to follow Him, and it demanded ultimate sacrifice on His part, to the point of laying down His life for our sakes. And even though in marriage the devotion of love is played out on a human level, its commitment is no less. We shouldn't expect it to be.

How do you see marriage as a picture of Jesus' relationship with the church?

_____

_____

_____

_____

Marriage is a blessing that God gives us for our benefit and joy. But it's also a blessing He intends to share through us with the world. Christian marriage is meant to be not just a gift for the participants but also a picture to the world of what God's love for us is like. That's a pretty big challenge! As Christians, the way that we love and serve our spouse is supposed to demonstrate the way that God loves and serves us. But love like that doesn't come naturally to us. Passively waiting, hoping, and dreaming for marriage is no way to prepare ourselves for the challenges that building a life together with another sinful human being will unavoidably bring. The only way we can be ready for marriage is by practicing now, with our family and friends, the principles of service, discipline, and sacrifice that marriage will require for the rest of our lives.

Great Love Stories: Jacob and Rachel

The Scene:
Read Genesis 29:10–20.

If you've read the entire story of Jacob's life recorded in Genesis, then you know that he wasn't really your typical idea of a saint. In fact, even though now he's remembered as one of the fathers of the faith, Jacob is one of those people whose story makes you wonder how he even got included in the Bible. Jacob is the poster child for sibling rivalry. He was a sneak, a thief, and a liar. His name actually means "deceiver," and he lived up to it. The only reason he was even at his uncle Laban's house, where he met Rachel, was because he had cheated his brother out of his father's blessing and had to run away from home to avoid his brother's vengeance. Although later in his life Jacob would experience several personal encounters with God that would deeply affect him, at this point in his story he is, at best, a very ordinary man.

What does Jacob do when he first sees Rachel?

_____

_____

_____

_____

Jacob's love story is a great example for us, because the heart of it is service. Jacob is just a regular guy—maybe even worse than average—but his first reaction when he sees Rachel is to serve her. He's just come on a long journey, running from home; he's tired and dusty, and it's not really his job to water his uncle's sheep, especially when he's just arrived as a guest. But he doesn't even think about that. The minute he first sees Rachel, he jumps to his feet to serve her. And this is the magic of romance; when we first fall in love, it's easy to serve. It becomes natural, because service is always the instinctive result of love. Jacob discovers that as he leaps to his feet and falls over himself opening the well and watering the sheep. Rachel must have watched in some amazement as he awkwardly urged the animals to drink, bashfully watching her out of the corner of his eye with a hunger for her approval. He was so infatuated with her that he was happy to work for her father for free, just for the chance to be around her. When Laban suggested paying him—something Jacob hadn't even thought of (and this guy is ordinarily the last person to forget his own interests)—the only thing Jacob thinks of is Rachel. You can almost hear his thoughts: "Money? *Payment?* For what? All I want is to be around her . . ." Seven years of service was a really high price for a bride in those days, but Jacob doesn't even realize that. In fact, he ends up gladly serving a total of fourteen years for Rachel's hand, and you never hear him complain about the length of time. It felt to him like only a few days, because "he loved her so much."

When has it been easy for you to serve?

_____

_____

_____

When is it hard for you to serve others?

_____

_____

_____

When we're in love, the reaction is the same. We want to serve our husband; it becomes incredibly easy to serve, and it's impossible to imagine that the desire to encourage and serve him could ever diminish. Time floats by in a blur, and we barely even notice. All we want is to be around him, and we're willing to make any sacrifice to make him happy. It would be nice if that state of mind really could last forever. But it doesn't.

Unfortunately, the passion to serve another that is so natural under the influence of early romance quickly becomes just as challenging and difficult as serving any of the ordinary people in our lives. In fact, sometimes serving your husband is a lot harder than serving anyone else, because your expectations of him are higher, and the pain of being disappointed by him is twice as bad. That is why the best way women can prepare to serve their spouses for the rest of their lives is by serving the people around us now—and the more challenging that person is, the better the opportunity for growth in service. How would it change your life if you began to consciously think of every difficult relationship as a chance to prepare yourself for marriage? Think of the most frustrating relationship in your life, the person who is most challenging for you just to be around, let alone to serve. What if you could think of that relationship as an opportunity to practice for the moments when your husband will disappoint and frustrate you, to serve that person as you would want to serve your husband? Not only would it transform your relationships now—but it would build a foundation of habitual service to others that is based on truth and commitment rather than feeling—a habit that would surely empower your marriage in incredible ways.

Who is hard for you to serve? How can you serve them this week?

_____

_____

_____

_____

How can you serve the people closest to you? Your family and closest friends? List three people and three specific ways you can serve each one.

_____

_____

_____

_____

What types of service are really hard for you? How can you make opportunities to do those kinds of service?

_____

_____

_____

_____

Quiz:
Are You a Servant?

How much have you already developed the discipline of service? Are you a selfish brat or a humble servant? Answer these questions to find out!

1. When you see someone drop all their books in the middle of a busy hallway, you:
    a. Laugh at them.
    b. Stop and help as long as you're not already running late.
    c. Drop whatever you're doing to help them pick up the books.
    d. Help them pick up the books and listen for an opportunity to talk with them about your faith while you're doing it.

2. When your friends want to go do something fun, you:
    a. Only go if they'll agree to an activity that you pick.
    b. Usually let someone else choose what you're doing; you just enjoy spending time with them.
    c. Always pick everyone up, because you're the only one with a car.
    d. Are always too busy to go.

3. When it comes to housework, you:
    a. Can't tell a dust rag from a mop.
    b. Help your mom out occasionally on the weekends.
    c. Regularly ask your parents if there are ways that you can help out.
    d. Do pretty much everything; you're in charge of all the housework around here!
    e. Do a lot of it but also help teach your younger brothers and sisters how to sort laundry.

Activity:
Get it Done!

Here are some more practical ideas for ways to practice service in your life right now.

- Fold and put away the laundry in your house.
- Wash the dishes.
- Baby-sit your younger siblings or younger neighbors for free.
- Walk someone's dog.
- Visit someone who is sick or elderly.
- Volunteer at a soup kitchen.
- Get a part-time job as a waiter at a restaurant (they'll give you free training on how to be a first-class servant!).
- If you can drive, call home when you're out and ask if you can pick up any groceries or run errands for your family.
- Write a friend a note to tell them something you appreciate about them.
- Buy your mom or grandmother flowers as a thank-you for being who she is.
- Tutor other students in a subject you're good at.
- Pick up trash in a park in your community.

My Experience of Service

After you've put your ideas into practice by doing one of the ideas listed, reflect on your experience by writing about it.

I enjoy serving others because . . .

_____
_____
_____
_____

Service is hard because . . .

_____
_____
_____
_____

I learned about myself that . . .

_____
_____
_____
_____

I learned about God that . . .

_____
_____
_____
_____

LESSON 10

Discovering "the One"

Reflect

"You don't know what life's going to bring you. Because of the fear of the unknown, for me to make those vows and have peace I had to know that this person was God's choice for my life."

—my friend, Kaneen

How do you choose your friends?

_____

_____

_____

_____

What are the three most important traits you want your future husband to have?

_____

_____

_____

_____

Thoughts

Most women have some idea of the personality traits, physical characteristics, and character qualities they're looking for in the man they want to marry. But for some of us, these general ideas can turn into shopping lists longer than a four-year-old's Christmas list! For others, they may be only vague ideas, open to change and compromise the minute someone shows an interest in us, even if we know that man doesn't meet the qualities we want in a relationship. I think it's good to balance the two, keeping a clear idea of what you want and what God wants for you but also staying open to surprises that God might choose to bring into your life. However, there are some things we should never compromise on in relationships. When you're considering spending the rest of your life joined with a man, there are certain character traits that you should insist that he have before you even consider a relationship with him.

What do you think is the single most important characteristic to look for in a husband?

_____

_____

_____

_____

_____

If I were to consider this question, I would have a hard time narrowing it down to just one characteristic. Obviously, if I'm going to commit my life to someone else for the rest of my life, then it's essential that he be a strong Christian with a godly character. But it's hard to narrow that generalization down to one characteristic. There are so many different qualities and actions that you have to observe in order to learn someone's character: their spiritual disciplines, their interactions with others, their reputation, and the way they react under pressure.

And in addition to the difficulty of choosing what characteristics to look for, it's also hard to know how much of a person's true character you're actually seeing at first glance. You have to know someone for a long time, in many different situations, before you can form any kind of accurate judgment on their character. Even then, it's hard to know how much of what you're seeing is real and how much is calculated to impress you—especially in a dating relationship. And with all the threats to marriage in our culture, with the divorce rate increasing every day, the thought that it's my responsibility to choose the right man can be completely overwhelming.

When I as a single woman try to narrow my "list" down to one or even a few characteristics that I should be looking for, it can be a challenge. However, many of the married couples whom I asked about this question came up with the same answer. Just like my friend Kaneen whom I quoted earlier, many of the married Christian women I've talked with agree: the single most important thing in choosing a husband is knowing that that this man is God's choice for you. His looks, interests, and even personality and character may change over time, as will your own interests, abilities, and needs. Only God knows what the future holds for you and for the man you marry. So the most important question you need to ask yourself in a relationship is not how well he matches up to your "shopping list" but how certain you are that God is calling you to be in that relationship with that man.

> "LORD, I trust you. I have said, 'You are my God.' My life is in your hands . . . ."
>
> —PSALM 31:14, 15 NCV

Only God knows our past and our future; only God knows all that we will be faced with in our marriage relationships and what we will have to deal with together with our spouses. Only God can choose the right husband for us, the man whom He is preparing for all that we will walk through together in the challenges of life. Only by trusting Him completely with the choice of our marriage partner can we be certain that our choice is a good one.

How can you listen to God's guidance regarding the man you date and marry?

_____

_____

_____

_____

Listening to God's guidance and understanding His will in our decisions is one of the most important things we can do as Christians. Living as a Christian doesn't just mean guessing what God wants us to do based on what we know and believe about Him, it also means discerning what He wants us to do in specific situations based on what He's telling us today. In order to do this, we have to make our personal, intimate, individual relationship with Him a priority. It's not enough to go to church and listen to what other people say about God—if you want to be able to understand what He wants for you in the important decisions of life, like who you'll marry, then you have to spend time every day learning to recognize His voice and understand His guidance.

How does God guide you in your decisions right now?

_____

_____

_____

_____

Can you think of a specific decision when you asked for God's guidance and felt certain that He answered you and directed you to what His will was?

_____

_____

_____

_____

What is difficult for you about listening to God and following His guidance daily?

_____

_____

_____

_____

Great Stories: The Wife of Noble Character

The Scene:
Read Proverbs 31:10–31.

Even though I think that having a list of everything you want in a spouse can sometimes prevent you from seeing what God is giving you, it's clear from this passage that there's nothing wrong with having high expectations. In fact, this list is far more specific and challenging than any list I've ever come up with! Although this passage is describing the ideal wife, the principles and character traits described here are just as valid for a husband. This passage provides us with a pretty solid picture of both the character qualities and the habits we should be looking for in a husband.

List three actions that the woman in this passage does habitually:

_____

_____

_____

List three character traits this woman exemplifies:

_____

_____

_____

Character is demonstrated in what you do. The ideal wife described in this passage demonstrates her character by her actions of service, prudence, and caring. She is hardworking, disciplined, trustworthy, and diligent. She is financially secure; she makes money and she invests it well. She is generous and caring; she takes care of both the strangers who are poor and her own household. She is reliable; her reputation commands respect, both for herself and for her family. She is wise and offers good advice to everyone.

This passage doesn't say anything about this woman's beauty. In fact, it says very little that our modern society would consider romantic. The list that the Bible gives us for the ideal spouse is surprisingly practical; it actually talks about her financial responsibility and hardworking diligence more than any other qualities. Many Christians would probably consider it shallow and worldly to evaluate a potential spouse based on their financial ability. However, I think the principle here is the idea of responsibility and respectfulness. This woman is worthy of respect in every way, in practical and physical matters as well as in wisdom and spiritual things. She has a strong reputation, and nothing she does will ever bring her husband disgrace or disrespect. He can count on her to represent their family well and to faithfully take care of both him and their children.

Although romantic emotions, physical attractiveness, and spiritual connectedness are important aspects of a relationship, it's also essential that we evaluate a potential husband in a practical matter. Don't look just at what he says about his spirituality or his feelings for you; evaluate him carefully based on his past and present actions.

Which of the qualities described in this passage do you believe are most important in a husband?

_____

_____

_____

_____

What qualities would you be willing to compromise on?

_____

_____

_____

_____

_____

What I'm Looking For

You probably already have a pretty good idea of the traits you're looking for in the man you want to marry. It's easy and fun to imaginatively invent your "ideal" husband! But don't make this list idly; that will only encourage your unrealistic expectations and maybe even make it harder for you to recognize the person God has chosen for you when he does come along. Instead, pray carefully about the character and calling you believe God is guiding you to look for in your lifetime match. Read through Scripture passages that describe godly men and women, and consider what traits are most important. Think through the calling you believe God has for your life, and consider what aspects of that calling must be shared by a man if you're to share your life with him. For example, I believe that God has called me to sing for His glory. I don't have to marry a man who's a singer, but I do have to marry someone whose own calling is compatible with mine. Someone who believes they are called to be a missionary shouldn't marry someone who never wants to leave their own country. What dreams and callings has God placed on your heart, and how would they have to match up with the man you're going to spend your life with?

I believe that God has called me to:

_____
_____
_____
_____
_____

I am praying for a spouse who lives a godly and holy life as demonstrated by these character qualities:

_____
_____
_____
_____
_____

Prayer

Lord, I pray for the man You have chosen for me to someday marry.
Although I don't know him, I know that You know everything about him. I
pray that You would keep him safe from physical, emotional, and spiritual
dangers. Please begin now to prepare him for marriage by . . .

Prepare me to meet him and love him by . . .

_____

_____

_____

_____

_____

_____

Grow this person to be like You, especially in Your . . .

_____

_____

_____

_____

_____

_____

_____

Amen.

LESSON 11

Understanding Forgiveness

Reflect

Forgiveness is not an option. If we belong to Christ, then God has forgiven us; therefore we have no right to not forgive others, or ourselves.

What is the worst thing you've ever been forgiven for?

_____

_____

_____

_____

What is the hardest thing you've ever had to forgive?

_____

_____

_____

_____

Thoughts

I once asked a friend, a strong Christian leader, what was the hardest thing he ever had to forgive. His reply was so poignant that I will never forget it. He told me that when he first met his wife, he knew she was the woman he wanted to marry. "But her story," he told me, "was not the story I had wanted for the woman I would marry."

73

Our stories—our past, our experiences, and our memories—are a powerful force in shaping who we are. I cannot imagine the pain of having to forgive the most important person in your life for a terrible betrayal. Your husband will have to live for the rest of his life with the actions that you take today. Likewise, you will have to live for the rest of your life with the actions and mistakes that your future husband commits today.

Forgiveness is one of the most difficult disciplines of the Christian faith. It never comes naturally to us. Human nature cries out for justice. Even when we make mistakes, we are uncomfortable with forgiveness, with undeserved mercy; we want to do something to make it right. The first logic of a two-year-old is always, "It's not fair!" There is a deep hunger in our nature for things to be fair.

"I will sing of your love and fairness; LORD, I will sing praises to you."
—PSALM 101:1 NCV

But the justice of God isn't much like our natural idea of justice. With the Cross, God turned justice on its head. In Christ, God punished the righteous so that He could freely forgive the guilty. No longer can we feel good about what we've done right or hope that our goodness will outweigh our mistakes in the scales of God's justice. Nor can we weigh others in our own scales, balancing their kindness to us against past mistakes and deciding what they deserve. The Cross opens the way, not only for God to forgive us, but for us to forgive others, freely and without reservation.

In Matthew 18:23–35, Jesus tells a parable about a servant who owed money to his master. The amount that he owed was equivalent to millions of dollars—more than he could ever hope to repay. But when the servant begged his master for mercy, promising to pay him back in time, the master inexplicably decided to forgive the debt entirely and let the man go, completely free.

It seems obvious that the servant ought to have responded with joy and gratitude. Instead, he went out and found another servant who owed him a few dollars. When the second servant couldn't pay the first, he had the man thrown into prison.

Later, the master heard what had happened.

"Then the master called his servant in and said, 'You evil servant! Because you begged me to forget what you owed, I told you that you did

not have to pay anything. You should have showed mercy to that other servant, just as I showed mercy to you.' The master was very angry and put the servant in prison to be punished until he could pay everything he owed.

This king did what my heavenly Father will do to you if you do not forgive your brother or sister from your heart."

—MATTHEW 18:32–35 NCV

In several other places throughout the gospels, Jesus tells us that if we don't forgive others, God will not forgive us (see Matt. 6:14, 15). God's forgiveness is undeserved, unearned, and free, but it wasn't cheap—it cost Him His life. We are called to forgive others just like God forgives us: free and undeserved, no matter what the cost is to us personally.

I believe this kind of forgiveness is something we must learn to extend to ourselves, as well. If God has forgiven you, then it's wrong for you to continue to wallow in guilt or self-hatred. God has set us free from sin and guilt, and He has freed us for a reason. He will redeem your story, no matter how difficult or impossible it may seem.

"God has freed us from the power of darkness, and he brought us into the kingdom of his dear Son. The Son paid for our sins, and in him we have forgiveness."

—COLOSSIANS 1:13, 14 NCV

To redeem means simply to buy back. No matter how far down your story or the story of someone you love has gone, God promises to redeem it—to buy it back from darkness, to transform it into something beautiful. The story of His own Son is a story of failure, of punishment, of loss, ending in persecution and death. But God transformed the cross, an instrument of torture and death, into the most beautiful symbol the world has ever seen: the symbol of resurrection, life, and forgiveness. That is exactly what God wants to do with our stories—to transform even the ugliest parts into a beautiful demonstration of His power and glory. Forgiveness is the means through which that happens; when we accept God's forgiveness for ourselves and offer it freely to others, then the door is opened through which the power of the Cross can enter our stories, transforming and redeeming them.

Great Love Stories: Hosea and Gomer

The Scene:
Read Hosea 1:2–11; 3:1–5.

What kind of woman did God tell Hosea to marry?

_____

_____

_____

_____

What did God tell Hosea to do after Gomer had cheated on him?

_____

_____

_____

_____

The story of Hosea and his wife is probably one of the most shocking stories in the entire Bible. Hosea was a man of God, a prophet, and a preacher who proclaimed God's Word. If anybody needed a wife who would be a supportive and godly woman of character, surely it was Hosea. And yet, God told Hosea to deliberately choose a prostitute for his wife—a woman with not only a history but a habit of infidelity. God told His chosen prophet to marry a woman who not only had already been unfaithful but whom he knew would be unfaithful in the future. Why would God want to put His prophet through the terrible pain of repeated unfaithfulness?

What reason does God give Hosea for His command?

_____

_____

_____

_____

Many times in the Old Testament, God told prophets to enact a picture of what God was teaching His people. Just as Jesus told parables illustrating

His teachings, in the Old Testament, God often used His prophets to act out stories in their lives, turning them into real-life parables illustrating God's message. That's exactly what God was doing with Hosea.

God wanted His people to understand how much it hurt Him when they betrayed Him. When we turn away from God, He feels exactly like a betrayed lover—confused, hurt, angry, deceived. God wanted Hosea to understand what He was feeling.

Even the worst betrayal a human could ever experience, such as the betrayal of a wife to her husband, doesn't compare with what we as God's creation have done to Him when we turn away from Him. And yet, God has already forgiven us. He gladly takes us back, just as He told Hosea to take Gomer back after she cheated. When we consider the depth of God's forgiveness toward us, it becomes a little easier to forgive.

Who do you need to forgive?

_____

_____

_____

_____

How can you accept the power of God's forgiveness for that person?

_____

_____

_____

_____

_____

Knowing I'm Forgiven

Even if you believe in God's forgiveness, it can be hard to feel it and trust it all of the time. How can you let the truth of God's forgiveness of your past sink into your heart and mind so that you don't have to live weighed down by guilt? The most powerful way is through Scripture. When Satan tells us lies about our guilt and condemnation, Scripture is our sword of protection, defeating lies and reminding us of the truth of God's forgiveness. Write the following verses on an index card, and re-read them whenever you feel doubtful of God's forgiveness. Memorize them, and then you'll never be apart from the promise of God's forgiveness.

2 Chronicles 7:14

_____

_____

Psalm 103:8–12

_____

_____

Psalm 130:4

_____

_____

Ephesians 1:7

_____

_____

1 John 1:9

_____

_____

Forgiving Others

There's a saying that says we should just "forgive and forget." But forgiving and forgetting are not the same thing. Forgiveness doesn't mean sweeping something under the rug and pretending it never happened. In Jesus' parable of forgiveness, before the master could forgive the servant, he had to know how big the debt was. Then he was able to cancel it. In the same way, we cannot truly forgive just by merely forgetting. In order to forgive, you must first acknowledge that a wrong has been done; then you must accept Christ's payment on the Cross for that wrong in place of the payment that person owes you. Christ died for the sins of the whole world—not just yours, but for all the wrongs that have been done against you as well. The means by which we can forgive others is the same means by which God forgives us—by accepting Christ's punishment as payment for that sin against us, thus allowing the person who deserves that punishment, who did that wrong, to go free, forgiven.

I have been wronged and hurt by others by . . .

Jesus, I know that You paid for those sins by Your death on the Cross. I accept Your payment for those sins in place of the people who deserve them. From now on, help me to demonstrate Your love and forgiveness to these people by . . .

Amen.

LESSON 12

Overcoming Fear

Reflect

Fear is one of the greatest obstacles to our fulfilling God's purpose in our lives. Especially when it comes to relationships, fear is often one of the main reasons why things don't go as they should. If we are living in fear, we are not really living.

What are your biggest fears about relationships?

_____

_____

_____

What situations tend to bring out your fears?

_____

_____

_____

Thoughts

You might be afraid to enter a new relationship because of a fear of repeating the past. You might be stuck in a series of bad relationships because you're afraid to be alone. Or you might be unable to open up in relationships right now because you're afraid of being known for who you really are, afraid of rejection.

Fear is a bondage that God never intended for His children. He created us to live in freedom and love, not bound by fear. No matter what your fear, it's not part of the way that God intends for you to live.

> *"I asked the LORD for help, and he answered me. He saved me from all that I feared."*
>
> —PSALM 34:4 NCV

As long as you are trapped by fear, you will not be able to enjoy the gifts God wants to give you. Fear is a kind of slavery; it stops an action before it even begins. And the more you give in to fear, the more you'll be bound by it.

What decisions have you made recently that were based in fear?

_____

_____

_____

_____

_____

We have an instinct for self-preservation. We don't want to place ourselves in danger, and we often see danger when it isn't really there. Because of this, it's easy for our lives to become dominated by fear. But the more we base our lives on fear, the more difficult it becomes for us to hear God's voice or see His guidance in our lives, and the more difficult it becomes for us to accept the gifts He is bringing into our lives.

> *"We know that in everything God works for the good of those who love him. They are the people he called, because that was his plan."*
>
> —ROMANS 8:28 NCV

We can overcome fear when we set our sights on the big picture. God is in control, and He can transform everything that happens in our lives—even the most frightening and painful events—into something good that contributes to His plans for us. When we remember that, then we don't have to be dominated by our fears.

Great Love Stories: Esther and the King

The Scene:
Read Esther 1:1, 2:18; 3:1—5:7; 7:1–10.

What reasons did Esther have to be afraid of the king?

_____
_____
_____
_____

What motivates Esther to overcome her fear? (See 4:12–16.)

_____
_____
_____
_____

Most of the time, we have a good reason for our fears. Our fears are often rooted in our own mistakes or bad experiences, but that wasn't the case for Esther. She hadn't done anything to put herself into a difficult situation; she had been chosen and placed there by circumstances completely out of her own control. First of all, she was Jewish, which meant that she was a member of an oppressed minority in a large empire. Secondly, the king of that empire, after having deposed his queen, held a beauty contest to find a replacement wife, of which Esther was the lucky winner. And while it was a great honor to be chosen as queen, King Xerxes wasn't exactly known for his kindness—after all, he had just divorced his previous wife for refusing to obey his every whim. So the advice that Esther's uncle, Mordecai, gave her, to keep her nationality secret and basically "keep a low profile," sounded like a wise choice to her.

But it wasn't long before Esther's nationality would become a central issue to the story. When Haman, the king's right-hand man, decided he wanted to kill all the Jews, Esther was faced with a terrible decision: she could try to keep her identity secret and hope to escape the massacre, or she could risk her own life by facing the king and leveling an accusation against one of the most powerful men in the kingdom. Can you imagine how Esther might have felt when she found out about Haman's plan? Her first response to the news (4:11) makes it clear that she immediately came to the same conclusion her uncle had: she was the only person who could have any chance of averting the disaster. However, she also knew that to even attempt to tell the king about the plot was to risk her life. For her to even approach the king without having been personally summoned was punishable by death, and she might easily be executed without even having the chance to tell the king her message and plead for mercy on her people, if not herself.

What would you do in Esther's position?

_____

_____

_____

> " . . . And who knows, you may have been chosen queen for just such a time as this."
>
> —ESTHER 4:14 NCV

It's her uncle Mordecai's advice that gives Esther the courage she needs. Although Mordecai doesn't mention God specifically, his meaning is clear: there's a bigger purpose behind these seemingly coincidental events in your life. Out of all the beautiful women in the kingdom, Esther had been chosen as queen. Only God could have placed her in such a powerful position at just the right time when her influence would be needed to save the lives of all the Jewish people. The remembrance that God is in control of her situation is what gives Esther the courage she needs to go to the king—and she succeeded in saving not only her own life but the lives of thousands of her people.

What does it mean to you to know that all the circumstances of your life have God's ultimate purpose behind them?

_____

_____

_____

_____

You may have fears that are connected to your past, fears of rejection or of repeating old mistakes. You may have fears that are rooted in your family and the mistakes that your parents made. But everything about your past, even the negative parts, have a role in God's plan for you (See Rom 8:28). Instead of being caught up in our fears, God invites us to see the big picture of what

He is doing in us and through us in our own lives and the lives of others. Esther never planned to be queen, but the very situation she was afraid of turned out to be the means God used to save her people. In the same way, although there may be things in your past or even your present situation that are not perfect, God can redeem even your fears. He is more powerful than anything we do, more powerful than any situation we find ourselves in.

"Jesus said, 'Don't let your hearts be troubled. Trust in God, and trust in me . . .' 'I told you these things so that you can have peace in me. In this world you will have trouble, but be brave! I have defeated the world.'"

—JOHN 14:1; 16:33 NCV

Fear doesn't have to control your life or your decisions. In fact, God commands us not to be dominated by fear.

> *"Remember that I commanded you to be strong and brave. Don't be afraid, because the LORD your God will be with you everywhere you go."*
>
> —JOSHUA 1:9 NCV

How can you overcome fear? Use this list as a starting point, and prayerfully add your own thoughts.

Face your fears: do things you're afraid of.

_____
_____

Share your fears with friends and ask them to pray for you.

_____
_____

Confess your fears to God.

_____
_____

Memorize Scripture passages about God's protection, trustworthiness and control, and remember them when you're afraid.

_____
_____
_____
_____
_____
_____
_____

Giving Fear to God

Lord, I know that You don't want for my life to be controlled by fear. I have been afraid of . . .

I know that You have control over my life, and I trust that You . . .

Please help me to follow Your guidance and not be enslaved by fear by . . .

Amen.

Notes

Notes

Notes

Notes

Notes

Notes

Notes

Notes

Notes

I want my NCV

The NCV rocks!

WHERE FAITH MEETS FUNCTION – NELSON BibleZines™, THE ORIGINAL

Visit us online at www.ThomasNelson.com